Moto and Me

and Me

My Year as a Wildcat's Foster Mom

By Suzi Eszterhas

Owlkids Books

I used to tell my mom that one day
I would live in a tent in Africa…

Contents

My Life in a Bush Camp

As a child, I used to tell my mom that one day I would live in a tent in Africa. So it was a dream come true when I headed to the Masai Mara, a wildlife reserve in Kenya, to photograph animals.

I had planned on staying for a few months but wound up living there for almost three years. It wasn't easy. When I first arrived at the camp, there was no electricity. For the first year, I used oil lamps for light and charged my camera batteries and laptop using my jeep battery. To shower, I had to heat water over the fire, pour it in a bag, and then hang the bag from a tree branch.

But I loved living in the camp because I was close to animals I'd always dreamed of seeing. Nearly every night I fell asleep to a chorus of animal sounds: lions roaring, jackals yipping, zebras stampeding, and more. One night, I woke to the sound of panting outside my tent and looked out to see the spots of a leopard as he slinked by.

During the day, lots of animals wandered in and out of camp: hippos, hyenas, and even a friendly bull elephant. Venomous snakes, like mambas and cobras, were fairly common, and sometimes they came into my tent. One night I had a close encounter with a spitting cobra on my desk!

But the most exciting animal encounter I had was with a tiny, helpless wildcat named Moto …

SOUTH SUDAN

ETHIOPIA

AFRICA

Lake Turkana

KENYA

UGANDA

SOMALIA

Lake Victoria

Masai Mara

INDIAN OCEAN

TANZANIA

People are not allowed to build or hunt on the Masai Mara, so wild animals can roam freely and safely there.

I lived in a tent, which was more spacious than it looks. Inside, it fit my bed, a trunk for clothing and gear, and a small desk.

This is Moto at six weeks.

Meet Moto

Moto is a serval, a type of small, spotted wildcat. Servals live in many parts of Africa. Moto's family lived on the Masai Mara's savanna, which is like a sea of grass. Besides servals, the Masai Mara is also home to large African animals like lions, elephants, and giraffes.

Huge grass fires are common on the African savanna, especially during the summer, when the weather is hot and dry. My story with Moto begins with one of these fires. As flames raged across part of the Masai Mara, animals ran and flew away to escape. But Moto and his siblings were tucked in a nest of grass, waiting helplessly for their mother to return from hunting and rescue them. The kittens were too small and too weak to escape on their own.

Moto's mother smelled the smoke and returned to her kittens. One by one, she grabbed them gently in her mouth and quickly carried them away from the fire. All except for Moto …

Fires actually help keep the savanna healthy. They kill insect pests and limit the growth of trees, allowing grasses to grow.

Moto Loses His Mom

To move her kittens to safety, Moto's mother had to cross a dirt road. While she was rescuing Moto, the sound of an approaching vehicle startled her. She panicked and accidentally dropped him on the road before dashing off to the side.

The vehicle was a jeep carrying tourists on safari. The driver stopped when he spotted the kitten alone on the road. Moto's mother was probably hiding nearby, waiting for the car to leave so she could go back and get her baby. But the tourists didn't see her. All they saw was a tiny, helpless kitten that seemed to be alone.

Wanting to help Moto, they picked him up and drove him to the ranger station. Rangers have the important job of protecting the animals in the reserve. They would know what to do.

It took hours for the tourists to reach the ranger station. By that time, the rangers knew there was no way of reuniting Moto with his mother. She would be long gone. Moto was only two weeks old when he got separated from his mom. There was no way he could survive on his own.

I gave Moto his name, which means "fire" in Swahili, the language spoken by most people living in the Masai Mara.

Serval kittens stay with their mother for eight to twelve months. Moto was only two weeks old when I got him, so we had a long road ahead.

Moto's Foster Family

The rangers knew I had spent a lot of time studying and photographing cats, including servals, so they asked if I wanted to be Moto's foster mother. It would be different from raising him as a pet. I would have to teach Moto how to survive in the wild on his own, so he wouldn't have to rely on a human forever. When he was old enough and ready, I would return him to the wild, where he belonged.

Moto was saddened by the loss of his mother, and for the first week, he cried out often. The most important thing for an orphaned baby animal is to feel secure, so I stayed right by his side and showered him with affection. As he got more comfortable with me, Moto became very snuggly and purred loudly when I held him. Purring meant he was happy, so I was happy too.

Wild servals are usually born into litters of two or three kittens, so I decided Moto needed a foster sibling. I gave him a plush toy named Mr. Ducky. When I couldn't be with him, Mr. Ducky kept him company. Moto loved his new "brother" and spent hours snuggling with him.

Hungry Moto

My first big challenge was learning how and what to feed Moto. Baby animals need to be well fed to survive. In the wild, a baby mammal like Moto would drink its mother's milk, which has just the right mix of everything it needs to grow healthy and strong.

I managed to get a bottle to feed Moto, but I wasn't sure what should be in the milk. So I did a little research and got advice from the rangers, a veterinarian, and a local wildlife rescuer. I mixed a special formula of cow's milk, eggs, fish oil, and vitamins. Moto loved it.

When Moto was especially hungry, he drank his milk really fast. Once, he drank so fast that he started to choke. He couldn't breathe and his tongue started turning blue. I was terrified!

I quickly called a veterinarian, who told me to turn Moto upside down and gently smack his back. It worked! Milk came gushing out of his mouth and he took a huge breath. I hugged Moto until he and I both calmed down. I whispered in his ear that I would always keep him safe.

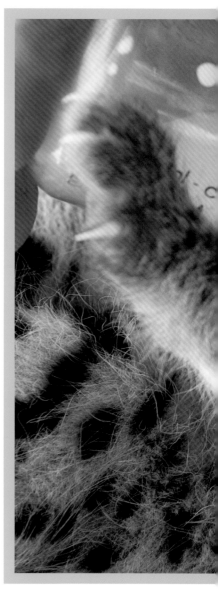

Moto was always hungry! I fed him every few hours. I even woke up a couple of times each night to give him a bottle.

Clean Kitten, Healthy Kitten

When Moto arrived, he was covered in fleas and ticks. Since he slept in my bed, I soon had them too. Fleas and ticks bite and can spread disease, so I wanted to get rid of them. Every day I plucked the tiny parasites out of Moto's fur with my fingers. It took weeks, but I didn't give up until every single one was gone.

Several times a day, I bathed Moto with a warm washcloth. This kept him clean, and it was also necessary to help him pee and poop. Kittens that young cannot go to the bathroom on their own. When their mom cleans their bottoms, the feel of her warm, wet tongue tells their bodies that it is time to go. The warm washcloth I used on Moto worked like a mother's tongue and helped him go.

After his bath, I always brushed Moto's fur using an old toothbrush. It was the perfect shape, size, and texture. It felt just like a mother serval's rough tongue.

A warm washcloth not only helped Moto go to the bathroom, it kept him squeaky clean too.

Moto couldn't get enough of the toothbrush!

Moto's First Adventures

For the first two weeks, Moto never left my tent. But as he grew stronger and more confident, he wanted to venture outside. I always kept a close eye on him to make sure he was safe.

Moto was shy but curious about the natural surroundings. He smelled the grass, listened to the birdcalls and other animal sounds, and watched everything with big, wide-open eyes. The first few times we left the tent, we would walk only a few feet before Moto retreated back inside, exhausted by his big adventure.

Moto learned about the world around him by sniffing, listening, watching, and climbing. It wasn't long before he was eagerly exploring far from my tent.

If a noise frightened him or he lost sight of where I was, Moto would call out to me. His call sounded like a short, loud meow. I'd return his call by saying "Moto," and he would answer back. Calling back and forth is how serval mothers and their kittens communicate when they cannot see each other in the long savanna grass.

Hearing Moto call for me felt good. I felt as if he saw me as his mother, and I knew I was creating a strong bond with him.

Moto had many adventures in the pouch, including a couple of rides in a bush plane.

Kitty Pouch

I was living in the Masai Mara game reserve to work as a wildlife photographer, so I couldn't just stay in my camp with Moto. I had to work. Every morning at sunrise, I drove off in my jeep to find animals to photograph on the savanna. This is called a game drive.

At first, I tried leaving Moto behind when I went on game drives, but he grew sad and lost his appetite. I had to find a way to bring him with me but still keep my hands free for taking pictures, so I had pouches sewn onto some of my shirts. I would put Moto in the pouch and carry him everywhere with me.

In the pouch, Moto could feel the warmth of my body and hear my heart beat. At first, he spent most of the time just tucked away inside, sleeping and resting. Later, when he got used to the pouch, he liked to ride with his head poking out, watching the world (and other animals) go by.

When I carried Moto in my shirt pouch, I felt like a kangaroo mom with her joey.

Hunting Mr. Ducky

At the age of six weeks, Moto started to play with Mr. Ducky the way a serval kitten in the wild would play with a sibling. He would stalk Mr. Ducky, pounce on him, and grab him by the neck. Playing like this helps serval kittens begin to develop their hunting skills. It meant that Moto's natural instinct to hunt and kill prey was starting to kick in.

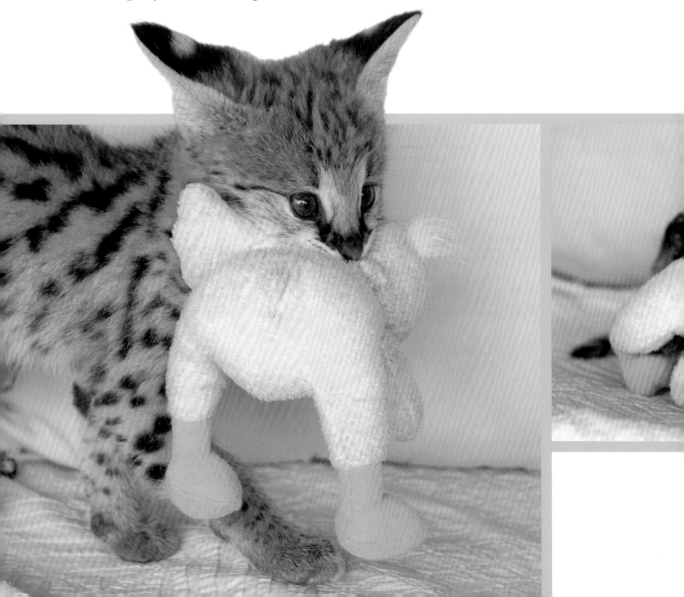

Of course, Moto's other playmate was me. He loved to surprise me and attack my shoes. (He loved shoelaces!) Sometimes he'd pounce on my leg or wrestle my hand. Moto's claws weren't very sharp yet and he still had his baby teeth, so it didn't hurt. These games were just pure fun. A wild serval kitten plays with its mother this way too.

Every time I saw Moto doing something that a serval would do in the wild, I was really happy. If he was going to survive on his own in the bush, he needed to know how to act like a wild serval.

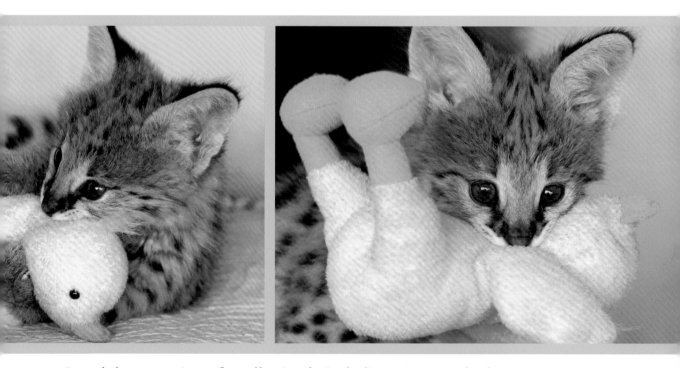

Servals hunt a variety of small animals, including mice, rats, birds, rabbits, lizards, insects, frogs, and fish. Mr. Ducky was about the same size as this prey, so he was perfect practice for Moto.

Moto's First Mouse

As Moto grew older, I began blending some chicken meat with his milk. I called it a chicken smoothie. He loved these smoothies and quickly preferred them to his regular milk. With his new taste for meat and his recent play hunting with Mr. Ducky, I knew Moto was ready for his first mouse.

In the wild, a mother serval brings dead mice to her kittens. The kittens enjoy their first taste of prey from the safety of their grass nest. In time, they learn to hunt for themselves.

On the day I gave Moto his first mouse, I wasn't sure what would happen. To my surprise, he knew exactly what to do. He grabbed it from my hand and hissed at me. Apparently he didn't want to share. Moto took the mouse right back to his nest—which was my bed! He devoured his prey in minutes.

Moto knew exactly what to do when he graduated from "hunting" Mr. Ducky to eating real prey.

Mice became Moto's favorite food.

Moto captures a piece of bark.

Moto the Wild Hunter

Adult servals are excellent hunters. They are known for their long, strong legs and incredible jumps. They can jump high in the air and land swiftly and silently enough to catch a mouse by surprise. It takes time to build up this strength and coordination, though, so when Moto was around four months old, it was time for him to start learning how to catch his own prey.

To become a hunter, Moto had to explore the bush on his own, without me watching over him. I started to leave my tent flap unzipped all the time, so Moto could come and go as he pleased. There weren't any fences around camp, and he could wander as far as he wanted. Sometimes he would disappear for hours. At first I worried about him, but he always came back.

Moto roamed freely in the bush around camp, practicing stalking, running, pouncing, and jumping. Soon he was catching mice, locusts, and lizards and bringing them back to me. I was very proud of him. Learning how to hunt was a huge step in being able to take care of himself.

After one hunt, Moto came back with a piece of bark to show me. I smiled and shook my head, thinking, "Silly Moto!"

Like all servals, Moto has very large, sensitive ears that are like radar dishes. Servals can hear small prey hiding deep in the grass or even under the ground.

When he hears a mouse in the grass, he pounces.

Moto hears something in the long grass. Is it food or a threat?

He plays with his prey.

And then he captures it!

Staying Safe

For Moto, one of the most important parts of growing up was learning how to protect himself. A serval's predators include lions, leopards, hyenas, and wild dogs. All these animals could be found around camp, and sometimes even in camp, so Moto got lots of practice learning to avoid them.

When he was frightened, Moto's natural response was to arch his back and puff out his fur to look bigger. All servals try to scare off threats this way. They also climb trees to escape predators, and Moto quickly became an excellent climber.

The first time I saw Moto in his defensive posture, I was impressed. He looked much bigger and fiercer than he really was.

Servals are most at risk of being attacked when they are in open areas away from trees. They have to rely on hiding in the savanna's tall grasses to avoid being seen.

Moto was naturally cautious in open areas. He spent a lot of time laying low in long grass. The spots on his coat helped him blend in with the sunlight and shadows in the grass, making him much harder to see.

Moto would scurry up a tree at the first hint of danger. Sometimes he wouldn't come down for hours.

Moto's first fishing lesson.

No More Milk for Moto

Until Moto was five months old, I gave him at least one bottle of milk a day. But then it was time to wean him off milk. Gradually, I gave him less and less, until he got none at all. Serval kittens in the wild are weaned when they are between four and seven months of age.

Moto was not happy about the loss of his milk. He whined loudly and batted me with his paws. To distract him, I gave him some special treats. One day I put a small catfish in a bowl for him. I wanted to teach Moto how to fish, since wild servals eat fish from time to time. At first he had no idea what to do with the catfish, and he spent a long time just batting it with his paws. There was a lot of splashing, but in the end, he caught it and ate it.

Without milk, Moto had to learn to drink water instead. It would be necessary for his survival in the wild. At certain times of the year, the Masai Mara is very dry. Servals must drink water whenever they find it.

At first, Moto was more interested in playing with water than drinking it. As he grew older, he learned to drink water regularly.

Moto on Safari

When Moto was a little kitten hanging out in my shirt pouch, he went with me on all my game drives. As he got older and grew big enough to be on his own, he usually spent his days at camp without me. But Moto still loved to ride in my jeep, so every once in a while, I would take him out on a game drive.

Together, we watched zebras, elephants, giraffes, and even cheetahs. Just as he did when he was a kitten, Moto spent hours gazing out the window at the different animals. I don't know why he was so fascinated. There were no fences at the camp, so he had seen all these animals before, with no glass between him and them. But Moto loved being on safari in my jeep, and I loved having him as my companion.

Some of my best memories from my time in Africa are the game drives I went on with Moto. I loved watching him watching the animals on the savanna.

Moto was strong and confident, and he could be very fierce.

Growing Independent

By the time Moto was eight months old, he was nearly the size of an adult serval. He weighed about thirty pounds (almost fourteen kilograms).

Occasionally, Moto still tried to play with me, but I wanted to avoid this. Now his claws were like razors, and he could be very aggressive. Sometimes he would get so excited that he would accidentally scratch my arms and face.

Moto didn't need much from me anymore. He could hunt for himself and clean himself, and he seemed able to protect himself from predators. Like a wild serval, Moto was becoming active at dawn, dusk, and nighttime. He slept most of the day.

But for a few minutes before he left to hunt each night, Moto still came into my tent. He jumped in bed and cuddled with me, purring loudly. Then he would hop off and quickly slip into the darkness outside. Even though I wanted him to be as independent as possible, I treasured those moments of cuddling.

Moto Returns to the Wild

Then one night, Moto didn't come to my tent. I woke up in the morning very worried. The day passed without any sign of him, and then the next and the next. I was terrified that something bad had happened to Moto. A leopard had been prowling around camp, and I feared the worst. I was heartbroken.

About a week later, I was driving near camp and spotted a serval. Moto! I called to him and he came to my jeep window and rolled around in the dirt. I knew this was Moto's way of saying hello. Over the next few weeks, several rangers who knew

Even though I missed Moto, I was thrilled that he had returned to the wild. It was everything I dreamed of for him.

Moto saw him too. He had made it! My job as his foster mom was done.

I returned to the United States about a year and a half after Moto returned to the wild. Although I don't live in Africa anymore, it still feels close. I cherish my memories of the bush camp, my game drives, and my time with Moto. I think of him all the time. I love to picture him hunting in the long grass of the savanna, under the African moon. But most of all, I like to think that Moto has become a father to kittens of his own.

All about Servals

- Servals are medium-sized wildcats found in Africa.

- Servals have a spotted coat that acts as camouflage, making their bodies difficult to see. This helps them stalk prey and hide from predators.

- Adult servals can weigh up to forty pounds (eighteen kilograms) and stand up to two feet (sixty centimeters) tall.

- Some people sell pet cats called Savanna cats, which are a cross between servals and domestic cats. These cats can be expensive and hard to care for. A better choice is to adopt one of the millions of stray domestic cats in desperate need of a home.

- Like most cats, servals are solitary, which means they live alone. The exception is serval mothers with kittens.

- Of all the cats, servals have the longest legs and biggest ears for their body size.

- Servals can use their long legs to run up to fifty miles (eighty kilometers) per hour and jump up to twelve feet (almost four meters) to catch birds in the air.

- Servals are incredible hunters. While most cats catch prey only 10 percent of the time, servals are successful about 50 percent of the time.

- Ancient Egyptians worshipped servals as gods. They appear on ancient Egyptian statues and other artifacts.

- Some servals have all-black coats. These are called melanistic servals. They look like small black panthers (which are actually melanistic leopards or jaguars). Melanistic animals have a special gene that causes them to produce more of a dark pigment, called melanin, in their skin and hair.

- In some parts of Africa, serval populations are at risk. Their savanna habitat is being destroyed by agriculture and development. In addition, many farmers kill servals because they sometimes prey on chickens. People also hunt servals for their fur.

To all the wildlife rescuers in the world, who work quietly and passionately to return animals to the wild.
— Suzi Eszterhas

Thanks to the Mara Conservancy, Kenya, and Terilyn Lemaire.

Owlkids Books acknowledges the financial support of the Canada Council for the Arts, the Ontario Arts Council, the Government of Canada through the Canada Book Fund (CBF) and the Government of Ontario through the Ontario Media Development Corporation's Book Initiative for our publishing activities.

Published in Canada by
Owlkids Books Inc.
10 Lower Spadina Avenue
Toronto, ON M5V 2Z2

Published in the United States by
Owlkids Books Inc.
1700 Fourth Street
Berkeley, CA 94710

Library and Archives Canada Cataloguing in Publication

Eszterhas, Suzi, author, photographer
      Moto and me : my year as a wildcat's foster mom / written and photographed by Suzi Eszterhas.

ISBN 978-1-77147-242-5 (hardback)

      1. Serval--Conservation--Kenya--Juvenile literature. 2. Wildlife rescue--Kenya--Juvenile literature. 3. Wildlife rehabilitation--Kenya--Juvenile literature. 4. Foster care of animals--Kenya--Juvenile literature. 5. Eszterhas, Suzi--Travel--Kenya--Juvenile literature. I. Title.

QL737.C23E898 2017   j599.75'2   C2016-905682-1

Library of Congress Control Number: 2016952800

Edited by: Niki Walker
Designed by: Barb Kelly

Manufactured in Shenzhen, China, in November 2016, by C&C Joint Printing Co.
Job #HQ4322

A   B   C   D   E   F

Publisher of Chirp, chickaDEE and OWL
www.owlkidsbooks.com
| Owlkids Books is a division of